TANKS

Andrew Kershaw

Illustrated by Doug Post,
Ross Wardle and Pete Robinson

A Piccolo Explorer Book

Below: Centurion Mk12. This British tank is fitted with an infra-red searchlight and infra-red driving lights so that is can operate at night.Below right: The Russian T-72 weighs 41 tonnes and carries a crew of three, a gunner, a driver and a commander. Its main gun is a 125-mm smoothbore.

Contents

About This Book

The tank is one of the most fearsome machines in modern warfare. Its thick steel armour protects its occupants from small-arms fire, and its caterpillar tracks enable it to cross rough ground at speeds of over 45 kph. Most tanks have a high velocity gun mounted in a revolving turret, and several machine guns or cannon. They carry a crew of two to six men, depending on the number of guns.

The first tanks, used by the British in the Battle of the Somme (1916), were clumsy and slow. Many of them broke down before they reached the enemy lines. But from them grew the deadly fighting machines of today.

Before the Tank

The Assyrians first began to develop fighting platforms during their wars of conquest from 1120 BC to 612 BC. These platforms became fast, lightweight battle chariots, which charged in formation at their opponents' infantry and cavalry.

By the end of the Middle Ages, cannons were playing an important part in battle. They were carried on to the battlefield on top of farm carts. Then, a man called John Zizka, combined farm carts and cannon to produce the first battle-wagons in 1419. They were a great success.

Many others, including Leonardo da Vinci, had ideas for armoured fighting vehicles. Leonardo's design for a covered vehicle capable of moving forward under enemy fire was produced in about 1500, but it was never built.

The Romans used battle chariots in the early days of their empire. Later, legionaries fought on foot or on horseback.

War elephants were used by the Romans and by Hannibal.

Assyrian chariots carried a driver, archer, and two shield bearers to protect them.

Leonardo da Vinci's idea for a combat vehicle was quite practical, unlike others of its time.

John Zizka's battle-wagons could be converted back to farm carts for use during peacetime.

The First Tanks

By 1915 millions of soldiers' lives had been lost in World War I. The British (and, quite independently, the French) realized that an armoured machine was needed which could cross trenches and save men's lives. Research into large-wheeled and tracked vehicles was already under way, but large-wheeled vehicles proved to be unworkable. In June 1915, two British engineers, Tritton and Wilson, tackled the problem of a tracked vehicle. A year later, the world saw its first ever tank battle when 50 of their Mark Is went into action at Flers.

Three weeks after they received the order for a tracked armoured fighting vehicle, Tritton and Wilson began construction of the first tank which became known as 'Little Willie'. It had no guns.

In 1912 De Mole designed a 'landship' and submitted his design to the British War Office. There was no response, despite the fact that the inventor had grasped the importance of all-round armoured protection, high ground clearance and the need for tracks. De Mole's design was very similar to that used in tanks built several years later.

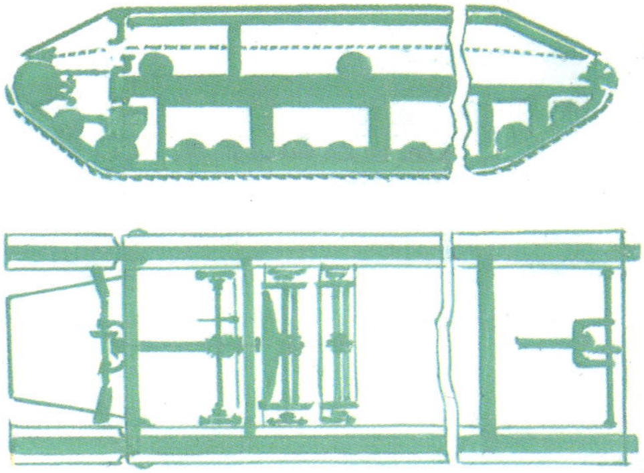

'Mother' was the first real tank. Earlier designs had too high a centre of gravity and too short a track length to cross broad trenches. Tritton and Wilson stretched 'Mother' to make the tracks longer.

Mark Is, the first fighting tanks, were almost identical to 'Mother'. Those that were fitted with five machine-guns were called 'Females' (left); those with 6-pounder guns were called 'Males' (below).

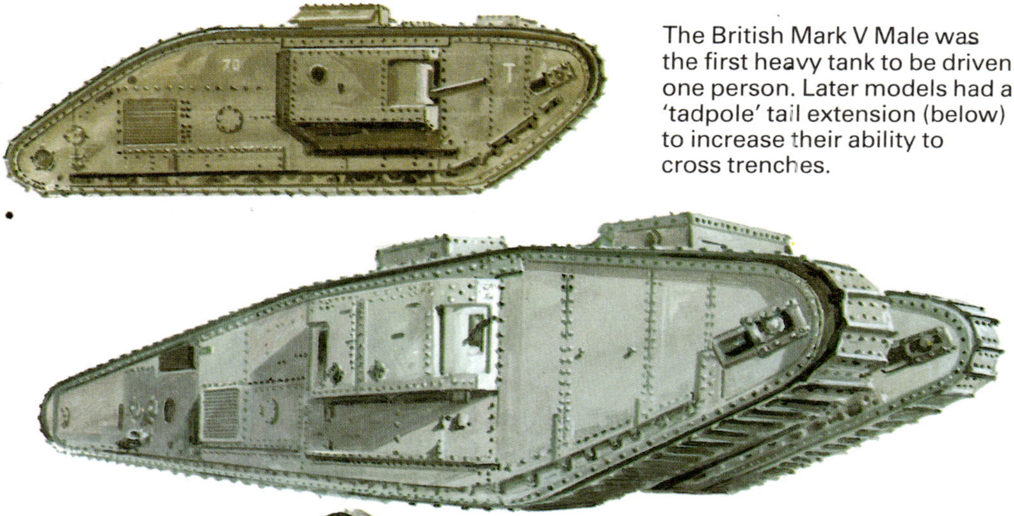

The British Mark V Male was the first heavy tank to be driven by one person. Later models had a 'tadpole' tail extension (below) to increase their ability to cross trenches.

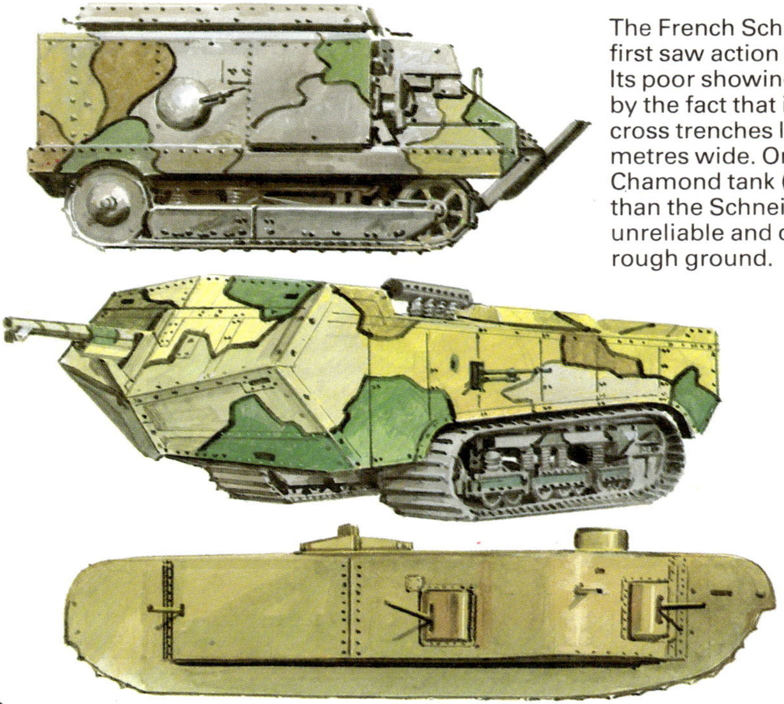

The French Schneider (left) first saw action in April 1917. Its poor showing was not helped by the fact that it could only cross trenches less than two metres wide. On paper, the St Chamond tank (centre) was better than the Schneider, but it was unreliable and did badly on rough ground.

The German K-Wagen (bottom) weighed 148 tonnes and was the heaviest tank of the time. However, these tanks were only completed after the end of World War I, when under the terms of the Treaty of Versailles they were all dismantled.

Tanks fought against each other for the first time ever on 24th April 1918 at Villers-Bretonneux. The German tanks are A7Vs, huge unwieldy machines with a crew of 18. The British tanks are Mark IVs, Female on the left, Male bottom right.

Between the Wars

Between 1918 and 1939 France and Britain competed against each other in selling tanks to other countries. But it was the British who produced the better designs. Variants of the Vickers Medium Tank and the later 6-ton A and 6-ton B were produced for the British army and for export.

In the meantime, Germany, which had been forbidden to develop any offensive weapons after World War I, was secretly doing just this. In 1934, their Panzer I was brought into service.

The French NC2 (1931) had a special suspension – double bogies supported by a coiled spring.

French AMC tank (1935)

The French Char D1 (right) of 1930 weighed 12 tonnes, had one man in the turret, one driving and one operating the radio and a machine-gun.

The American T1E1 light tank of 1929 (left) was not very successful.

The British Vickers Medium Mark II was one of the most successful tanks of its time. It weighed 13.5 tonnes and had a crew of five. Its main armament was a 47-mm gun and it carried 6 machine-guns.

Tank designers have always struggled to achieve the perfect balance between firepower, protection and mobility. Some of the results of their work between 1918 and 1939 are shown on these pages.

The German Pzkpfw 1A (above) had twin machine-guns in its turret.

American Medium A (1922)

American Combat Car M-1

British light tank Mark III

The British cruiser tank A-9 was not very successful. Its armour was only 14 mm thick.

Russian T-26C

Inside the Tank

Each person in a tank, whether it carries a crew of two or six, has an important job to do. Guns have to be loaded and fired, someone must maintain contact with the outside world, a mechanic must be on hand to make any necessary repairs, and the vehicle has to be expertly driven over sometimes hazardous ground. Lastly, the commander has a job to do as well.

All these tasks take place in cramped conditions. But conditions inside a modern tank are far better than those in the dirty, smelly, dangerous ovens of the past, when the crew faced serious injuries as part of their jobs.

The diagram on the left shows the limited angle of fire of a tank's own anti-tank gun. In combat situations uneven ground also affects the angle of fire, as shown in the diagrams below and right.

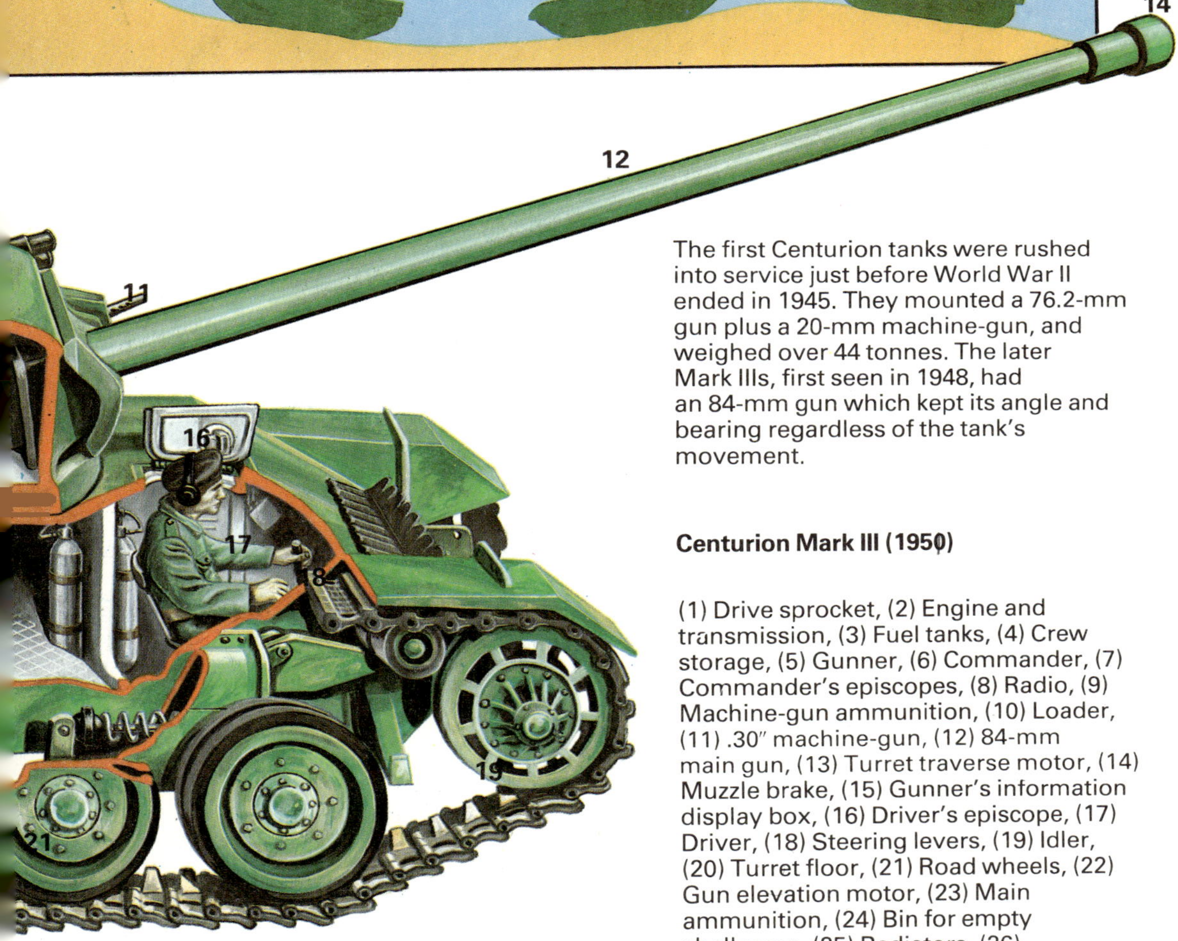

The first Centurion tanks were rushed into service just before World War II ended in 1945. They mounted a 76.2-mm gun plus a 20-mm machine-gun, and weighed over 44 tonnes. The later Mark IIIs, first seen in 1948, had an 84-mm gun which kept its angle and bearing regardless of the tank's movement.

Centurion Mark III (1950)

(1) Drive sprocket, (2) Engine and transmission, (3) Fuel tanks, (4) Crew storage, (5) Gunner, (6) Commander, (7) Commander's episcopes, (8) Radio, (9) Machine-gun ammunition, (10) Loader, (11) .30″ machine-gun, (12) 84-mm main gun, (13) Turret traverse motor, (14) Muzzle brake, (15) Gunner's information display box, (16) Driver's episcope, (17) Driver, (18) Steering levers, (19) Idler, (20) Turret floor, (21) Road wheels, (22) Gun elevation motor, (23) Main ammunition, (24) Bin for empty shellcases, (25) Radiators, (26) Armoured exhaust.

The Desert War

Tanks seemed to be ideal for war in the desert. With their broad tracks and all-round manoeuvrability they could go where wheeled armoured cars and other vehicles could not go. However, it soon became clear that the army with the best and the most tanks would win the desert war.

Italian-occupied Libya soon fell to the British simply because the British Infantry Mk11 tank, *Matilda,* had superior armour and a higher speed than the Italian M-13/40 tanks. But before long, Rommel and his Afrika Korps arrived to aid the Italians, and soon Libya was in German hands. Rommel's Panzer Mk111s sacrificed heavy armour for speed, and quickly showed their superiority over the ageing British machines.

However, by November 1941, a new generation of British tanks, which included the Valentines and Crusaders, were being produced. So too were the American Stuart light tanks, the M-3 General Lee and General Grant tanks, and, later on, the M-4 General Sherman. Germany quickly retaliated by sending newer versions of Panzers and their Tiger tank. But they were too few to stem the flood of Allied tanks.

The deserts of North Africa became the battlefield for many fierce tank battles.

Matilda II (right) was designed by the British in 1938. It won many battles in 1940 and 1941, but quickly became outdated. Its armour was 78 mm thick, and it carried a crew of four.

The Italian M-13/40 weighed 14 tonnes and carried a crew of four. Its armament was a 47-mm and 3 machine-guns. This tank was found to be too slow for desert warfare, and many of them fell into British hands.

Battle Tanks

By 1939, the Germans were concentrating their armour in special armoured divisions made up of tanks, artillery, infantry, engineers and administrative services.

With their hard-hitting Panzers, Panthers and Tigers, they thought they were all set to win the war. But the tank war in Europe was won by the Americans, British and Russians. Sherman, Churchill and T-34 tanks were produced in tens of thousands, and victory was eventually won by sheer weight of numbers.

Germany's Panther D (right) weighed 43 tonnes and carried a crew of five. Its heavy armour was 120 mm thick and its main armament a 75-mm gun. The tank below is a French AMX (1938).

The tank on the right is the American M-26 Pershing. It had a speed of about 50 kph.

The British Valentine tank (left) first saw action in the Western Desert in 1941.

The Russian KV-1 (right) was a successful battle tank. Its heavy armour was 106 mm thick and it could travel at 40 kph. The KV-1 weighed 46 tonnes and carried a crew of five.

The tank on the right is a French FCM (1936). Below is an American Locust tank which weighed only 8 tonnes. It was designed to be landed from the air into battle with its crew of three.

The German tank on the right is a PzKpfw 11L (Lynx). Below is a British Covenanter. This tank proved unsuccessful and was never involved in a battle.

In 1941, the Russians launched the T-34/76 (below) against the Germans. It was one of the best tanks of World War II. It weighed 28 tonnes and had 60-mm armour.

Germany's Tiger 1E (left) was one of the most powerful tanks of World War II. It weighed 56 tonnes, had armour 100 mm thick and carried an 88-mm gun. The great weight of this tank made it difficult to manoeuvre.

After the War

After World War II, arms sales boomed. The leading tank producers, Russia, America, Britain and France, made tanks which could fight in tactical nuclear wars. The British produced the Centurion. Its successors are still in use today. The T-54 was Russia's most important development. It contained complicated gunnery devices and night-fighting aids. In 1949 the French brought out the AMX-13.

Meanwhile, the Americans, who had held back in regard to tank development, had to improve on their Pershing design when they were faced in the early 1950s with the Russian T-34/85s of the North Korean army.

The American Patton II M-48 (right) was an improvement on the Pershing. Then came the M-60 (below). It had a British 105-mm gun.

To avoid being outgunned by the German Panther and Tiger tanks, the British produced the comet (below). It went into service between March and May 1945 to enjoy a short but successful career.

The Russian T-62 tank (below) appeared in the mid-1960s. It has a crew of four, a driver, a loader, a gunner and a commander.

The tank on the right is the British Conqueror. Below is the Russian T54D which carries night-fighting aids. The first T54 appeared in the late 1940s. It is fast and manoeuvrable and carries a 100-mm gun. There is a crew of four.

Below is the British Centurion, a powerful tank now fitted with a 105-mm gun. Its armour is 152 mm thick and it weighs 50 tonnes.

Modern Tanks

Some people may think that modern tank development should produce a new kind of tank, but traditional shapes and designs have to be improved first. Many modern tanks can travel under water. They also have an infra-red searchlight for night combat and variable suspension to suit all kinds of ground and firing positions.

In battle, modern tanks try to co-ordinate their movements with that of the infantry. This is done either by a pre-arranged plan or by on-the-spot radio conversations. Many modern tanks can be carried by air and can be flown directly to the area where they are most needed.

On the right is the French AMX-13. This is a light tank designed to be carried by air. The American M1 Abrams (below) is the first tank to be powered by a gas turbine engine instead of a diesel engine.

On the right is the German Leopard II. This tank has a powerful engine and good cross-country mobility.

The American Sheridan M551 light tank is armed with a Shillelagh, a rifled gun firing either high explosive shells, or a radio-controlled guided missile.

The French AMX-30 below has a speed of over 60 kph and carries a 105-mm gun. It weighs 34 tonnes.

On the right is the British Chieftain 2. The German Leopard I below is fitted with a British 105-mm gun. Although less powerful than Leopard II, a great number of these tanks are still in service.

Many tanks in front-line service today have special features. The latest model of the Russian T-72, for example, has armour panels which automatically spring out from its sides to protect it against missiles. The British Challenger fires a type of shell which can penetrate any known armour. The Israeli Merkava is designed for desert warfare.

As well as its protective panels, the latest model of the Russian T-72 shown below has additional silencers on its main guns.

The British Challenger below weighs 60 tonnes. It has a maximum speed of 56 kph and can cross trenches up to 3 metres wide.

On the right is the Israeli Merkava. Unlike most tanks it has a special emergency escape hatch at the rear for the crew.

Glossary

Armour It is essential that the tank's crew and the vehicle's vital parts are protected from enemy fire as much as possible. So, as weapons improved, the steel plate used in tank armour became tougher and thicker. In some tanks the armour plate makes up more than half the total weight of the vehicle. Its thickness can be over 200 mm (about 8 inches).

Caterpillar tracks These are a chain of metal plates that allow the tank to cross very rough ground and climb and descend slopes of 35 degrees. The metal plates encircle the tank's wheels and make a continuous track for the wheels to travel over.

Drive sprockets The wheels that are driven by the tank's engine. They engage with the caterpillar tracks and so drive the vehicle. Most tanks now have rear-sprocket drive.

Idlers The wheels at the opposite end of the tank to the drive sprockets.

Infra-red Infra-red rays are like light rays, but they cannot be seen by the human eye. Any object gives off infra-red rays in relation to its temperature. Modern tanks carry infra-red equipment that allows the crews to 'see' the enemy in total darkness.

Panzer The German word for armour. It came to mean 'tank' as well as tank divisions.

PzKpfw This German designation is short for PanzerKampfwagen. PzKpfw 1 was the first of all the Panzers. It came into service in 1934.

Smooth-bore gun These guns have no rifling inside the barrel to make the shell spin and keep it steady in flight. Instead they have ammunition with fins that steady the shells.

Suspension systems These are the various systems that absorb the shocks sent through the tank by the tracks' passage over the ground. Some have coiled springs, others leaf springs.

Turret The armoured structure on top of the tank which carries the crew, the guns and other equipment. It can usually be rotated.

Index